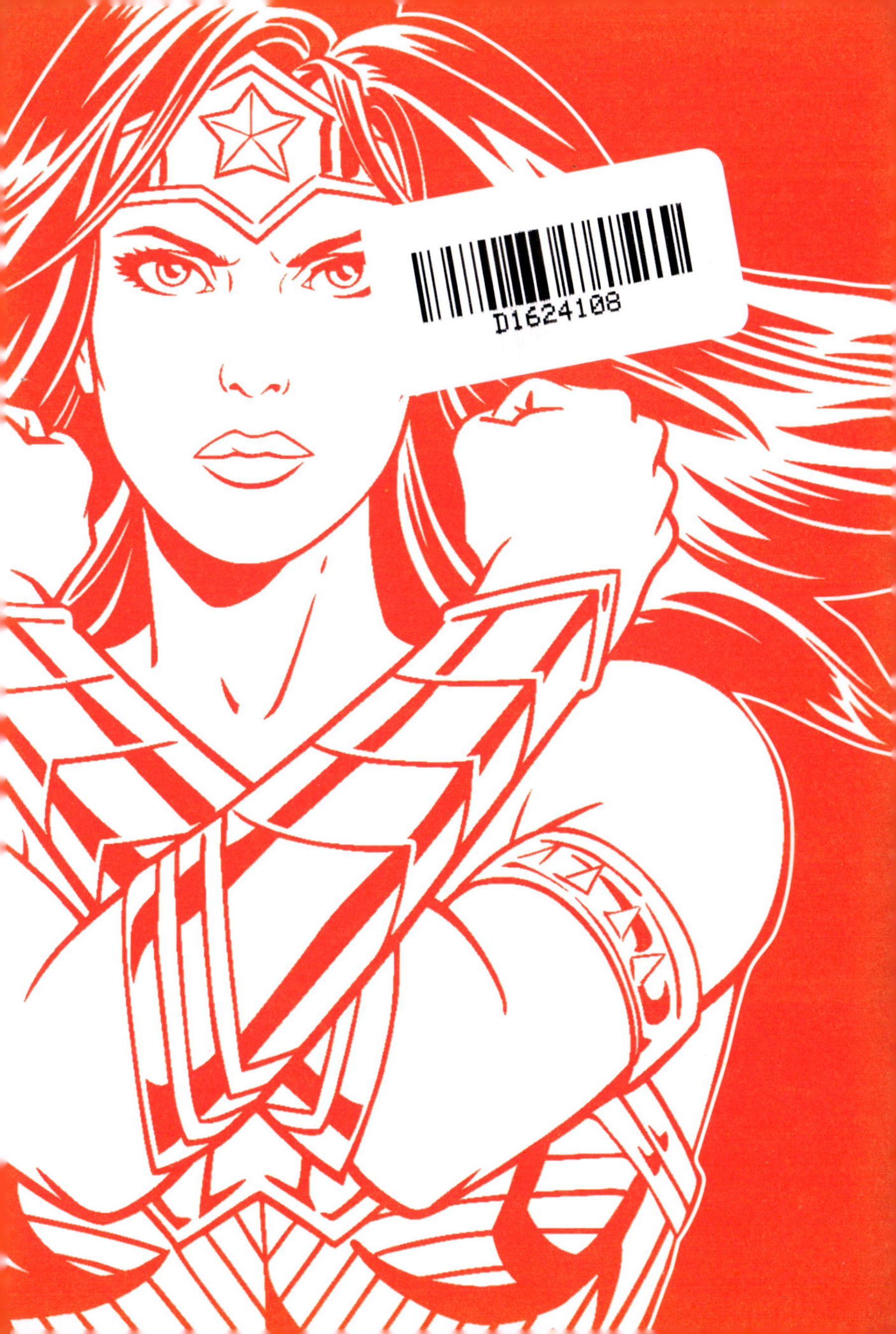

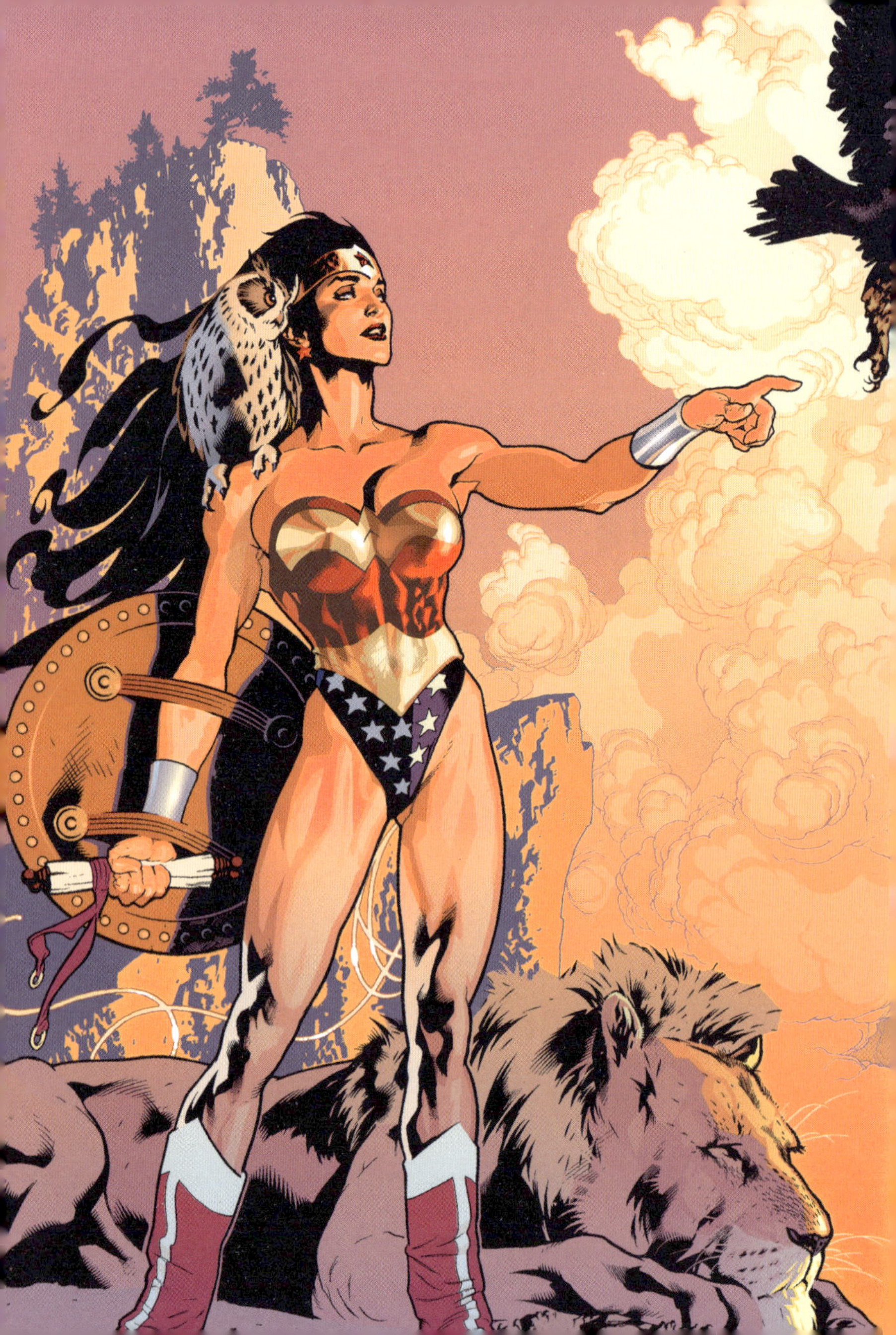

DC

BE MORE WONDER WOMAN

WRITTEN BY CHERYL RICKMAN

Wonder Woman created by William Moulton Marston

CONTENTS

FIND THE WARRIOR INSIDE YOU

Today it feels like we need Wonder Woman like never before. More than just a villain-catching, world-saving Super Hero, she is a noble warrior, one who protects the values humans hold dear: truth, justice, peace, and hope. Most of all, she represents the power of femininity—responding to aggression with compassion, speaking up with courage, and leading with emotional intelligence.

We all have a warrior inside us. If you want to know how to choose love over hate, courage over fear, and hope over despair, wonder no more. Wonder Woman will show you the way!

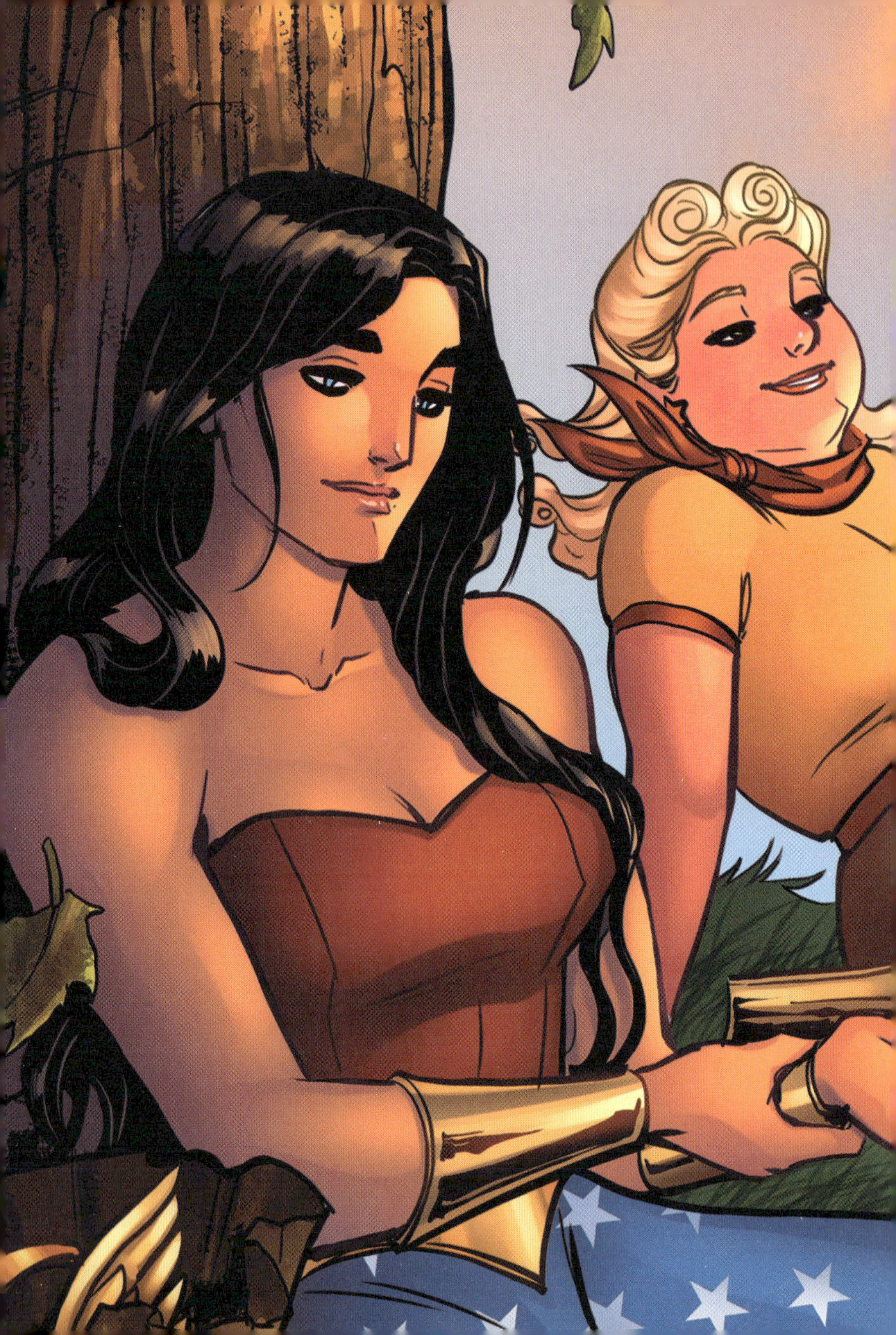

OTHER PEOPLE MATTER

The company you keep is important. Companions provide a sense of belonging, shape your beliefs, and have the power to lift you up—even when you're very different, like Wonder Woman and Etta Candy. So choose your companions wisely, and when you've found them, treasure them!

"No matter how small an act
of kindness or generosity or simple
positivity you put out into the world,
it will make a difference."

Wonder Woman

BE KIND

You might not be able to actually fly like Wonder Woman, but being kind can make your heart fly and your spirits soar. Kindness and positivity are contagious. They create a ripple effect that can inspire those around you. Helping others increases your own feelings of strength, makes you feel good, and reduces stress. What's more, the endorphins released provide a "giver's glow" and a sense of togetherness. So give your imaginary tiara a bit of a shine, then carry out a few acts of kindness and bask in that wonderful glow. And remember: if someone is kind to you, pay it forward.

"We have a saying, my people.
Don't kill if you can wound, don't wound
if you can subdue, don't subdue if you
can pacify, and don't raise your hand
at all until you've first extended it."

Wonder Woman

TRY COMPASSION FIRST

Fighting should be a last resort. Even on the brink of conflict, look for a way to defuse the situation and deflect negativity. Trying compassion first will not stop every battle before it starts, but it can help limit the damage. Fighting gods and witches such as Ares or Circe may have required Wonder Woman to use force, but she was able to lead with compassion when battling Strife and The Cheetah. Be like the Ambassador of Peace. Make compassion the first weapon in your armory.

"When we fight for what's right,
we never fight alone."

Wonder Woman

WE'RE IN THIS TOGETHER

Wonder Woman believes people are better united
than divided. Together, we can work for the common
good. With a little goodwill, barriers often simply
melt away. So why not make a decision to encourage
rather than compete? Replace comparison with
compassion. Share ups, downs, and wisdom.
Get to know people from different backgrounds;
their worlds may not be as strange and faraway as
Wonder Woman's homeland, Themyscira, but they
could still open your eyes to new ways of thinking.

"If it means interfering in an ensconced, outdated system, to help just one woman, man, or child... I'm willing to accept the consequences."
Wonder Woman

PEOPLE MATTER

Connection is at the heart of what it means to be human. However right you think you are, it's never all about you. Everyone wants to feel seen, heard, and valued. So honor all voices by listening well; give people your full attention, maintain eye contact, ask questions, and show an interest. Then, like Wonder Woman, have the courage to speak for those voices that struggle to be heard. If a cause matters to you, commit to doing something—anything—to help.

"Those in need must always
have access to alternatives;
they must always have hope."
Wonder Woman

GIVE HOPE

Hope helps you cope. A positive outlook lets
you put problems into perspective and rise above
difficulties. Hope enables people to bounce back
after challenges, enhances problem-solving abilities,
and bolsters resilience. And, as Wonder Woman
knows only too well, hope can turn a battle around
at the eleventh hour, even when all seems lost.
So, wherever you go, be a beacon of hope to others.
Help them open their minds to new possibilities
and fresh ways of pushing past obstacles.
It's the greatest gift you can give.

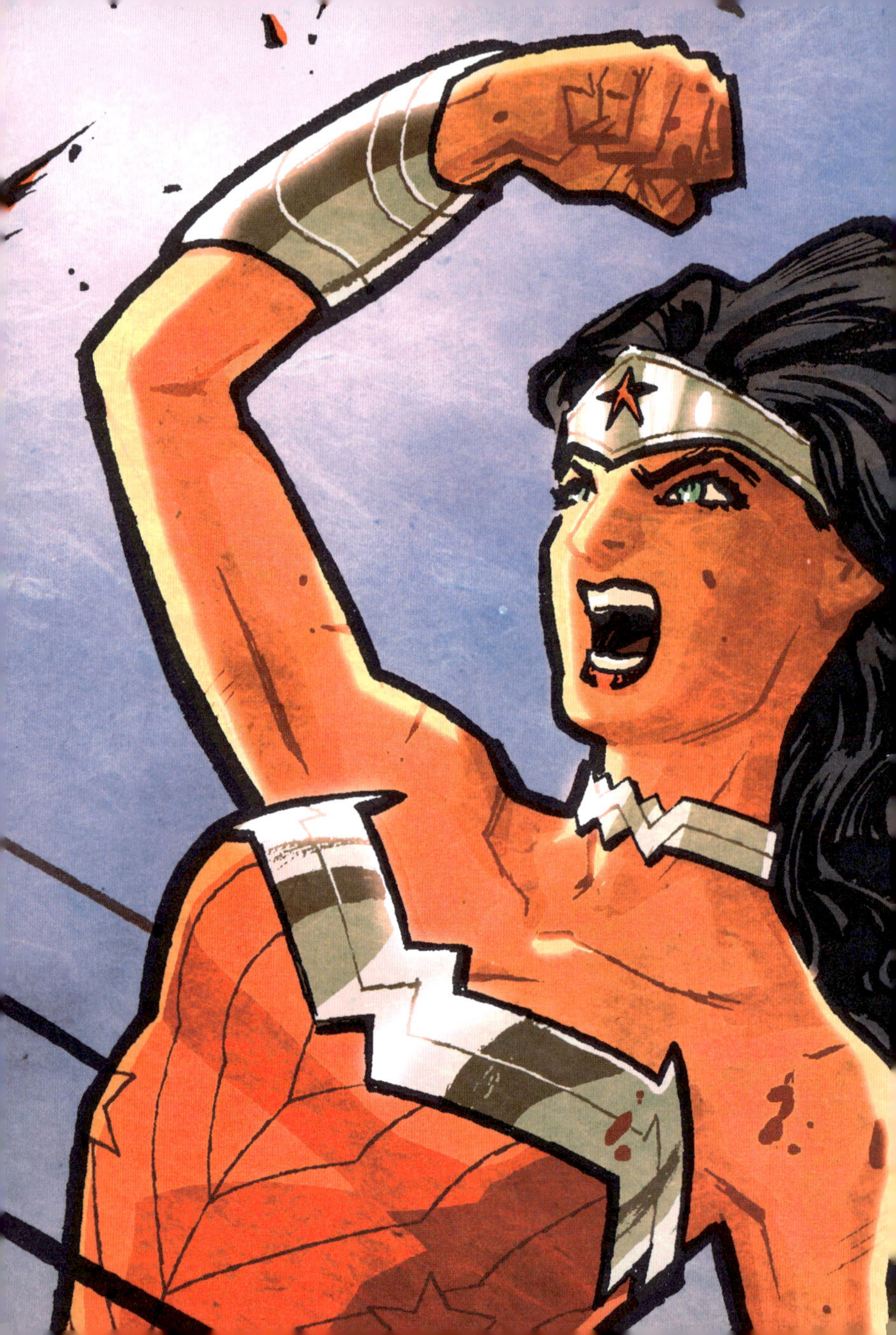

BE YOUR OWN SUPER HERO

Wonder Woman doesn't wait for others to start the fight for what she believes in—she leads the charge. Be your own Super Hero. Look for ways you can make a difference, and then go out into the world and put your magnificent Super Hero self to good use.

"All you have to do is have confidence in your own strength."

Wonder Woman

BELIEVE IN YOURSELF

Consider what makes you uniquely you.
Is it your humor, curiosity, creativity, or courage?
Perhaps people admire your leadership, humility,
persistence, or integrity? We all have unique
superpowers. Making the most of your individual
character strengths can boost well-being and
performance and build a buffer against stress.
So forget your flaws and focus on your fortes!
Start looking for ways to use your strengths
in your daily life.

"People never know what they're capable of, Diana dear. Even a bird sometimes has to be shown it can fly!"

Queen Hippolyta

DON'T UNDERESTIMATE YOURSELF

As we grow older, we start to compare and despair and feel like we don't measure up to expectations. Try not to fall into that trap. Wonder Woman believes in our power to do good and keeps pushing us to do what we can to claim that power. Consider the tough times when you've overcome obstacles you never thought you could. Then hold your head high and step into your superpower! Your capabilities are much greater than you think.

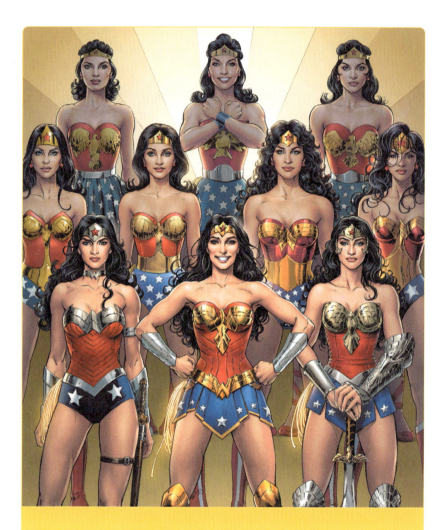

"How we see ourselves
is who we become."

Wonder Woman

YOU ARE ENOUGH

All anyone can do is be the best version of themself. Even Wonder Woman! Don't let yourself be eaten up with envy or bitterness when you meet someone who is a little better than you at this or that. Instead, work on accepting that you are enough and appreciated exactly as you are, flaws and all. Of course, the desire to improve can be a great driver, but it's wise to balance your ambition for who you hope to become with appreciation for who you already are. Don't worry what people think of you—that's outside of your control, anyway. Just be your bold, beautiful, bodacious self!

"If this is a warning... I defy it!"
Wonder Woman

CULTIVATE COURAGE

Wonder Woman's abundant energy allows her
to act in bold ways. You can be emboldened too,
by taking a risk now and then. Decide whether you
stand to gain more than you lose—and if you do,
go for it! Daily life gives us plenty of opportunities
to be brave, even if for just a few seconds, whether
it's mustering the courage to ask someone on a date,
speaking up to your boss, or facing an old fear. So try
that bold hairstyle or audition for that talent show.
Quiet that nagging voice of doubt and
step out of your comfort zone.

"Be creative.
Be adventurous. Be original."
Wonder Woman

DANCE TO THE BEAT
OF YOUR OWN DRUM

Do you sometimes struggle to fit in? If so, you aren't
the only one! It can be tempting to mask your true
self and follow others rather than go in your own
direction, but in the long run it's exhausting.
Instead, try going your own way and following
your own truth. Ignore any criticism from others;
eventually you will gain more respect. By celebrating
your individuality you can reduce the pressure of
social comparison and be free to get on with being
yourself. Wonder Woman has never been afraid
to dance to her own wonderful drumbeat.
What does yours sound like?

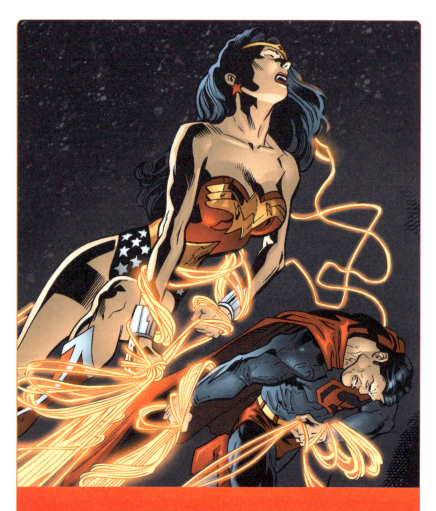

"Carry that courage and faith just a little further now."

Wonder Woman

PERSIST

One of the greatest traits of Wonder Woman
as the world's preeminent female Super Hero
is her dauntless energy, grit, and determination
to do whatever it takes to succeed. Follow her lead;
keep going when you feel like quitting, focus on why
you want to achieve your goal, and avoid distractions
and comparisons. If the task seems too big, break
it down into mini-milestones and take small steps.
Remember, the only sure way of failing
is to stop trying!

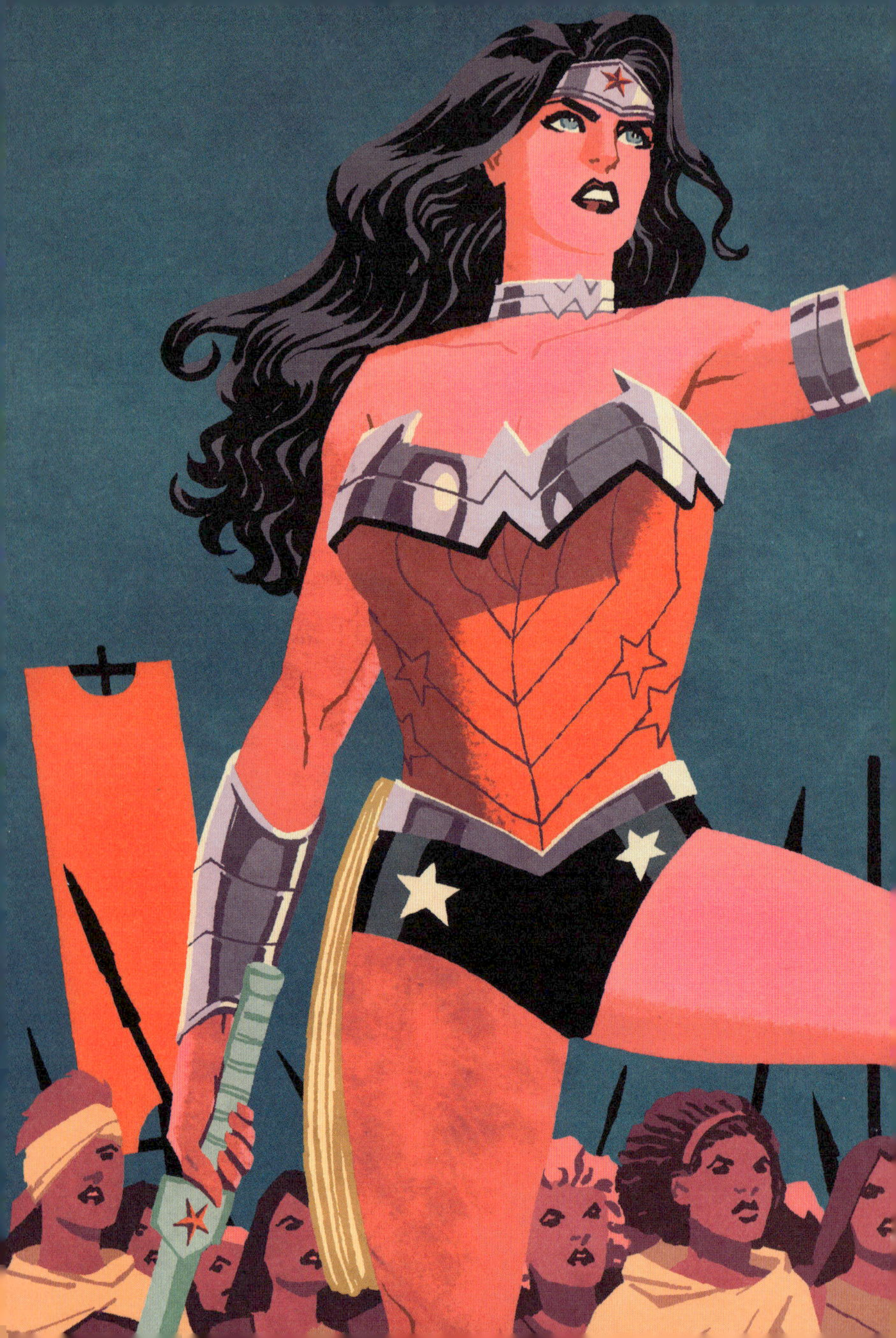

HONOR YOUR VALUES

Obstacles can seem less daunting when they stand between you and an ideal. That's because we're motivated by purpose. The values we hold dear and the changes we hope to make in the world get us fired up and give our lives meaning. So take up your metaphorical sword, find a cause, and fight for it!

"Oh, Gods of Olympus! Though I love Paradise, I yearn for more from my life. I yearn for purpose!"

Wonder Woman

FIND YOUR PURPOSE

What is your aim in life? What sparks your interest,
stirs your dreams, and motivates you to take action?
That's your purpose. A purpose is a strong guiding
force that provides a sense of direction in life.
Your purpose may not be saving the world, like
Wonder Woman's (although it could be helping to
save the rainforest). You might long to make a
medical breakthrough, lead a political party, write
a best-selling book, or just be the best you can be.
Whatever it is, get up, get out, and go for it!

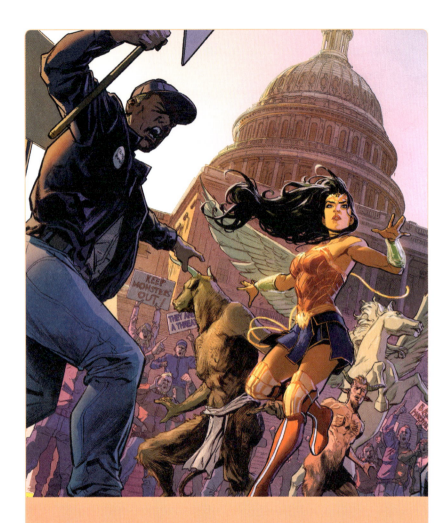

"What sort of world
do you want to live in?"
Wonder Woman

LEAD THE WAY

Wonder Woman wants to live in a peaceful world, where citizens of Earth are treated equally and with respect. What kind of world do you want to live in? What can you do to make it happen? Perhaps you want to live in a waste-free world or one where pollution is a thing of the past? These can seem like impossible goals, but know this: we are not powerless. So take responsibility, speak out, and above all practice what you preach.

"We have to live by
some sort of principle."
Wonder Woman

STICK TO YOUR PRINCIPLES

What values do you hold most dear? Kindness?
Politeness? Integrity? Before you try to influence
others, ask yourself whether the way you live your
own life reflects these values. It's all too easy to
come up with excuses, so ask yourself whether
you're truly sticking to your principles. Be honest
with yourself! Wonder Woman probably isn't around
to give you a whirl with her Lasso of Truth, but
a long, hard look in the mirror should suffice.

"League! All together!
We can do this!"

Wonder Woman

JOIN FORCES

Having a purpose is great. What's even
greater is finding others who share that purpose.
There's strength in numbers, and goals can usually
be achieved more quickly when there's a whole
posse pushing for them. So as you go about your
life, be on the lookout for like-minded people.
You don't have to form a formal team or organization
like Wonder Woman and the Justice League.
Maybe you just want to meet up with them now
and then to chat or exchange contacts.
Who knows, maybe they will open your eyes
to different ways of going about things.

"I cannot preach hate and warfare when I am a disciple of peace and love!"

Wonder Woman

LOOK AFTER EACH OTHER

If you had a magic wand (or a Lasso of Truth), what would you change in society? Who would you wish to protect? And how far would you be prepared to go to achieve your goals? Purpose and passion are great, but beware of letting a too-fiery sense of justice lead to feelings of hatred for those who oppose you. That's a fast way of becoming the very thing you despise. Like Wonder Woman, fight the good fight to make the world a better place for everyone… together.

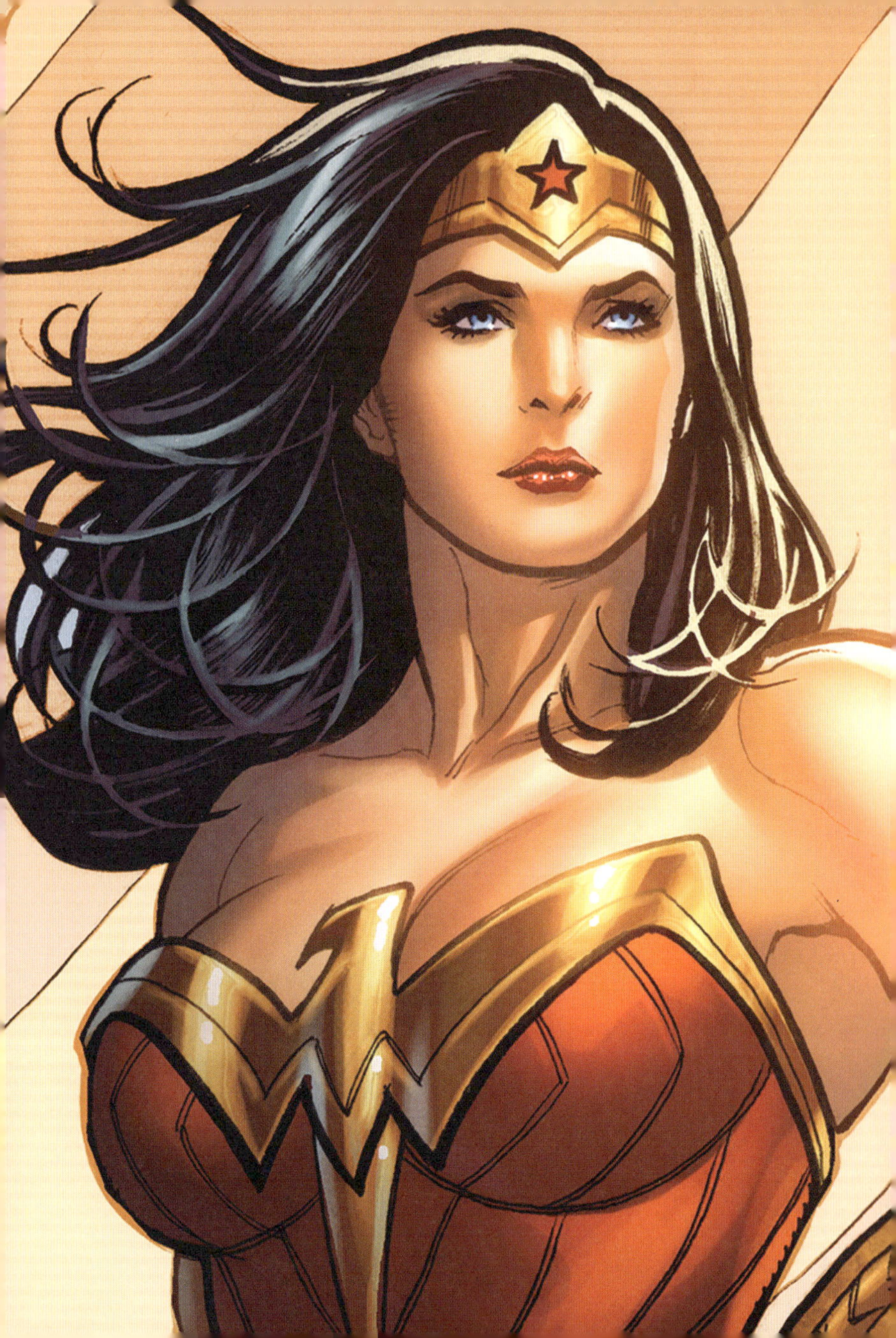

CHOOSE HOPE
AND CURIOSITY

Wonder Woman loves her family deeply. When Steve Trevor was stranded on Themyscira, Wonder Woman set judgment aside and welcomed this mere human into her world—then into her heart. As a result, she discovered a new kind of love. There are many ways to find and show love. Live your life with curiosity and hope too, and let in wonder, fascination, and love.

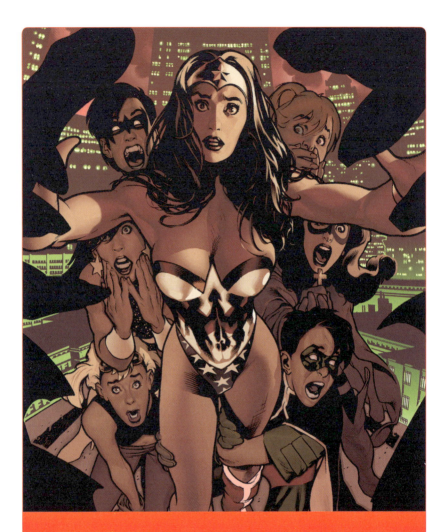

"Which will hold greater rule over you?
Your fear or your curiosity?"

Wonder Woman

BE CURIOUS

When ruled by fear, it's easy to be scared of
what people might think, which can stall creativity.
When ruled by fear, it's easier to say "no" to
experiencing anything outside your comfort zone,
even though those experiences could have been
the best of your life. Fear pushes you to stay safe
but live small, but that's only useful when you are
protected from REAL dangers, not imagined ones.
Curiosity is a superpower. It leads you to try new
things and experiment; to create, experience,
and live. Choose curiosity.

"Goodbye, mother. I am frightened.
Yet, I shall remember the power
within me whenever I think of you."
Wonder Woman

CHANNEL POSITIVITY

Wonder Woman treasures her loving connection with her ancestors. Not just her mother, Queen Hippolyta, but generations before—after all, they made her the Super Hero she is. When faced with uncertainty, you can do the same. Imagine all those who have loved and supported you being there to cheer you on. Use this empowering image whenever you feel unsure of yourself, then go forth and be fabulous!

"Love can exist with hatred,
each preying on the other."
Wonder Woman

FORGIVE

Sometimes it's easier to hate than to forgive,
but harboring animosity can make you feel ill.
When you dwell on what someone has said or done,
you waste energy on something outside your control.
You can't change the past; all you can do is respond
well. When you forgive, you regain control of a
situation and become a master rather than a victim.
Wonder Woman has forgiven The Cheetah's repeated
attacks, and in return The Cheetah has shown
glimmers of kindness to Wonder Woman. By forgiving
people (including yourself), you'll show your nobler
side and set a good example for others.

"When given choices, should we not choose love above all else?"

Wonder Woman

LOVE YOURSELF

Nobody's perfect—we're all just doing our best.
In a world that seems to promote self-doubt, liking
yourself can feel like an act of rebellion. But what's
wrong with being a rebel? When you choose love
over hate, there is no better place to start than with
yourself. Take time out to focus on yourself.
Find ways to celebrate and promote your own
uniqueness. Love yourself, and you'll soon
find that feeling rippling out to others.

"Remember, this man's world of yours will never be without pain and suffering until it learns love, and respect for human rights."

Wonder Woman

THINK OF OTHERS

Whenever you are frustrated by a long line
or you're being jostled in a crowded place, look at
people nearby. What do you think might be going on
in their lives? It's easy to forget that there are billions
of people on this planet, and each one has their own
burdens, expectations, and troubles… just like you.
So be patient and think kind thoughts. Wonder Woman
doesn't give up on the world, and neither should you.

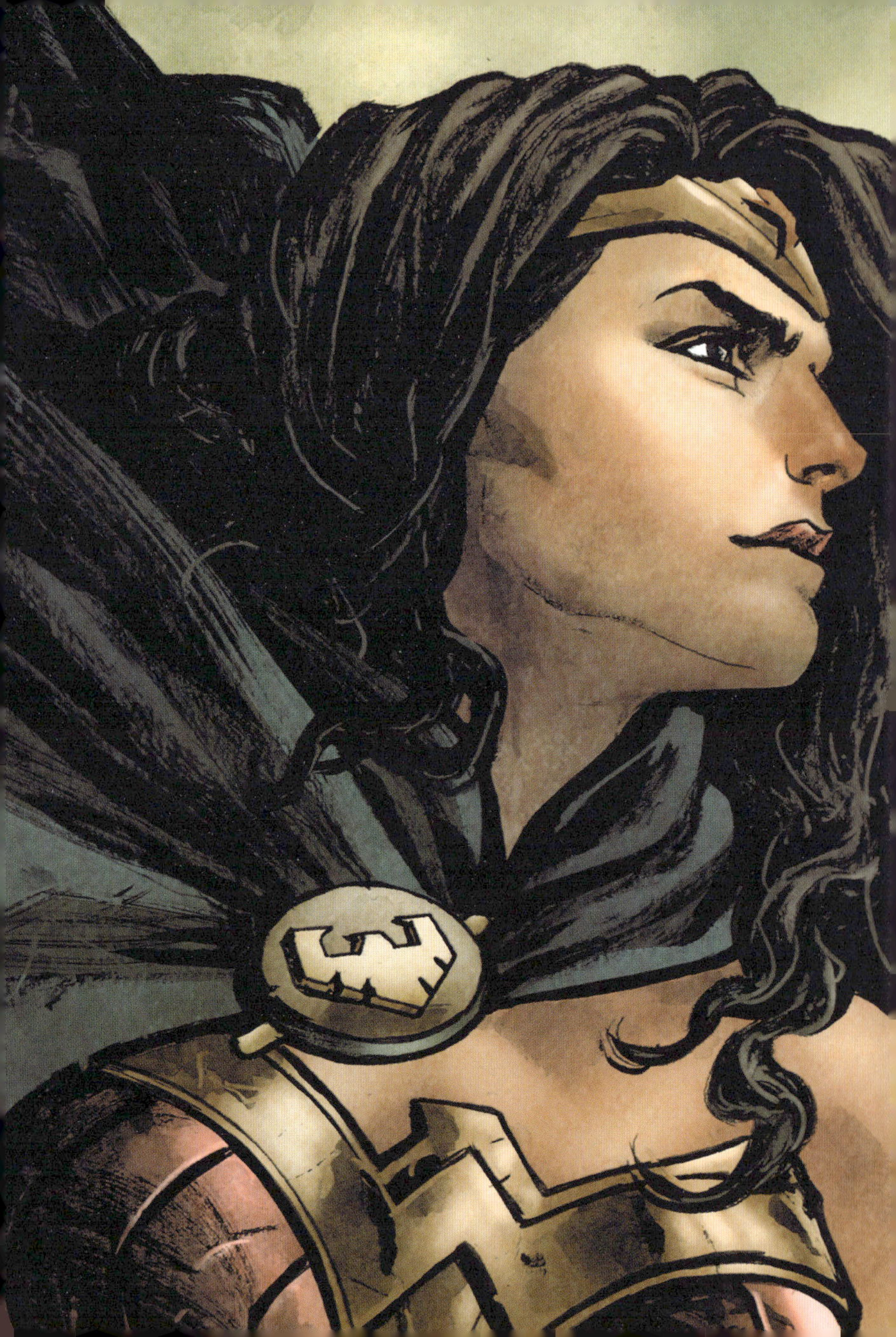

STAY OPEN TO LEARNING

Not even Super Heroes believe they know it all. Thinking you know everything can be dangerous, especially when you're battling with devious villains such as Angle Man or Doctor Cyber. Complacency closes you off to learning. In reality, the only failure is failing to learn from mistakes by repeating them over and over again.

"We are our pasts,
Barbara Ann."

Wonder Woman

LEARN FROM
YOUR MISTAKES

Everyone strives to remove flaws, avoid mistakes, and achieve perfection. How ironic when mistakes are the very things that help you learn fast and improve quickly. Mistakes are nothing to be ashamed of. Even Super Heroes make them! Wonder Woman failed to prevent her friend Barbara Ann Minerva from becoming The Cheetah. Instead of beating herself up, Wonder Woman resolved to learn from the experience, and held onto hope that Barbara might yet be freed from the curse. See your mistakes as the wonderful teachers they are. They show you what not to do next time.

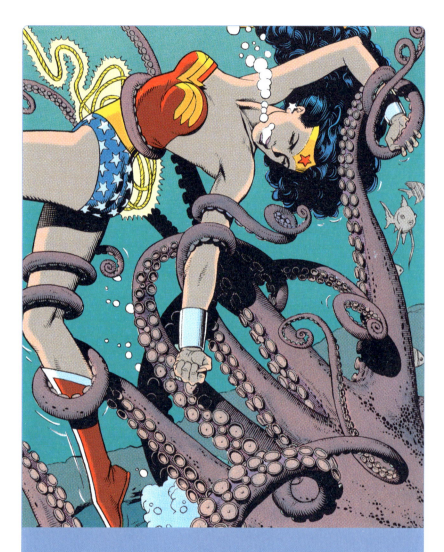

"Learn from their bad example."
Wonder Woman

DON'T LET OTHERS BRING YOU DOWN

Mean people can seem like monsters, trying to drag you down in a tangle of trouble, spite, and cheap shots. Maintaining integrity and decency when those around you are being hurtful (or, in Wonder Woman's case, trying to destroy you and the world) can feel like an effort of Amazonian proportions. But it's far better to maintain the higher ground and be nice in the face of unkindness. Be proud you are not stooping to their level; proud to be you and not them. Stay cool, stay classy, and shrug off their bad example. They just won't be able to keep a hold on you!

"It takes real character
to admit one's failures..."
Wonder Woman

ACCEPT YOUR FLAWS

Nobody's perfect, not even Wonder Woman!
Viewing yourself in a positive light only when
you're doing well isn't sustainable. Accepting your
imperfections makes for a much happier life.
So give yourself and everyone around you permission
to be human and cultivate a compassionate response
to getting things wrong. Have self-compassion,
which is different than self-esteem, because, with
self-esteem we feel good only when we succeed.
Self-compassion works when you fail, too.

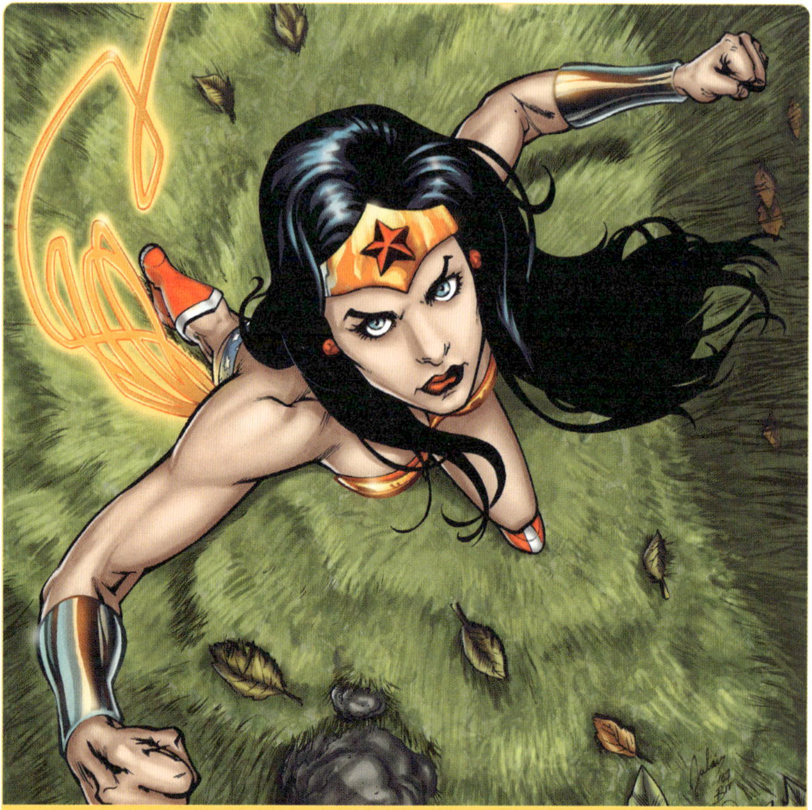

"A new journey to be started. A new promise to be fulfilled. A new page to be written. Go forth unto this waiting world with pen in hand, all you young scribes, the open book awaits."

Wonder Woman

WRITE YOUR OWN FUTURE

Wonder Woman allows us to see our own unique
potential for heroism. She represents autonomy—the
freedom to carve our own path. So, rather than
let other people (be they peers, family, teachers,
or the media) control your beliefs and shape how you
show up, decide to be the author of your own story!
Then tap into your inner hero, fix your eyes on your
goal, and plot your desired journey. The future is a
blank page just waiting for a brand new chapter.
It's up to you, and you alone, to write it!

Penguin
Random
House

Project Editor Pamela Afram
Editor Julia March
Editorial Assistant Victoria Armstrong
Senior Editor David Fentiman
Project Art Editor Chris Gould
Production Editor Siu Yin Chan
Senior Production Controller Louise Daly
Managing Editor Sarah Harland
Managing Art Editor Vicky Short
Publisher Julie Ferris
Art Director Lisa Lanzarini
Publishing Director Mark Searle

DK would like to thank: Benjamin Harper and Josh Anderson at Warner Bros.
Consumer Products; Benjamin Le Clear, Michele Wells, and Leah Tuttle at DC Comics.

First American Edition, 2020
Published in the United States by DK Publishing
1450 Broadway, Suite 801, New York, NY 10018

Page design copyright © 2020 Dorling Kindersley
Limited
DK, a Division of Penguin Random House LLC
20 21 22 23 24 10 9 8 7 6 5 4 3 2 1
001–320967–May/2020

A catalog record for this book is available
from the Library of Congress.
ISBN: 978-0-7440-2445-6

DK books are available at special discounts when
purchased in bulk for sales promotions, premiums,
fund-raising, or educational use. For details,
contact: DK Publishing Special Markets,
1450 Broadway, Suite 801, New York, NY 10018.
SpecialSales@dk.com

Printed and bound in China

A WORLD OF IDEAS:
SEE ALL THERE IS TO KNOW
www.dk.com

ARTIST ACKNOWLEDGMENTS
Raul Allen, Ross Andru, Brian Azzarello, Darryl
Banks, David Baron, BIT, Brian Bolland, Laura Braga,
Cullen Bunn, Jim Cheung, Cliff Chiang, Vicente
Cifuentes, Gerry Conway, Tony S. Daniel, Renae De
Liz, Tom Derenick, Ray Dillon, Mike Esposito, Nathan
Fairbairn, Romulo Fajardo Jr., Wayne Faucher,
Sebastian Fiumara, Sandu Florea, Jenny Frison, Yvel
Guichet, Don Heck, Hi-Fi Design, Bryan Hitch, Nansi
Hoolahan, Adam Hughes, Phil Jimenez, Joelle Jones,
Robert Kanigher, Joe Kelly, Jim Lee, Julian Lopez,
Aaron Lopresti, Eric Luke, Emanuela Lupacchino, Doug
Mahnke, Laura Martin, Patricia Martin, Marta
Martinez, Ray McCarthy, Jesús Merino, William
Messner-Loebs, Tomeu Morey, Tom Nguyen, Steve
Orlando, Sean Parsons, Borja Pindado, Mark Propst,
Alex Ross, Greg Rucka, Nicola Scott, Trevor Scott,
Liam Sharp, Gail Simone, Alex Sinclair, Dietrich Smith,
Scott Snyder, J. Torres, G. Willow Wilson, Matthew
Wilson, Xermanico

The publishers have made every effort to identify
and acknowledge the artists whose work appears
in this book.

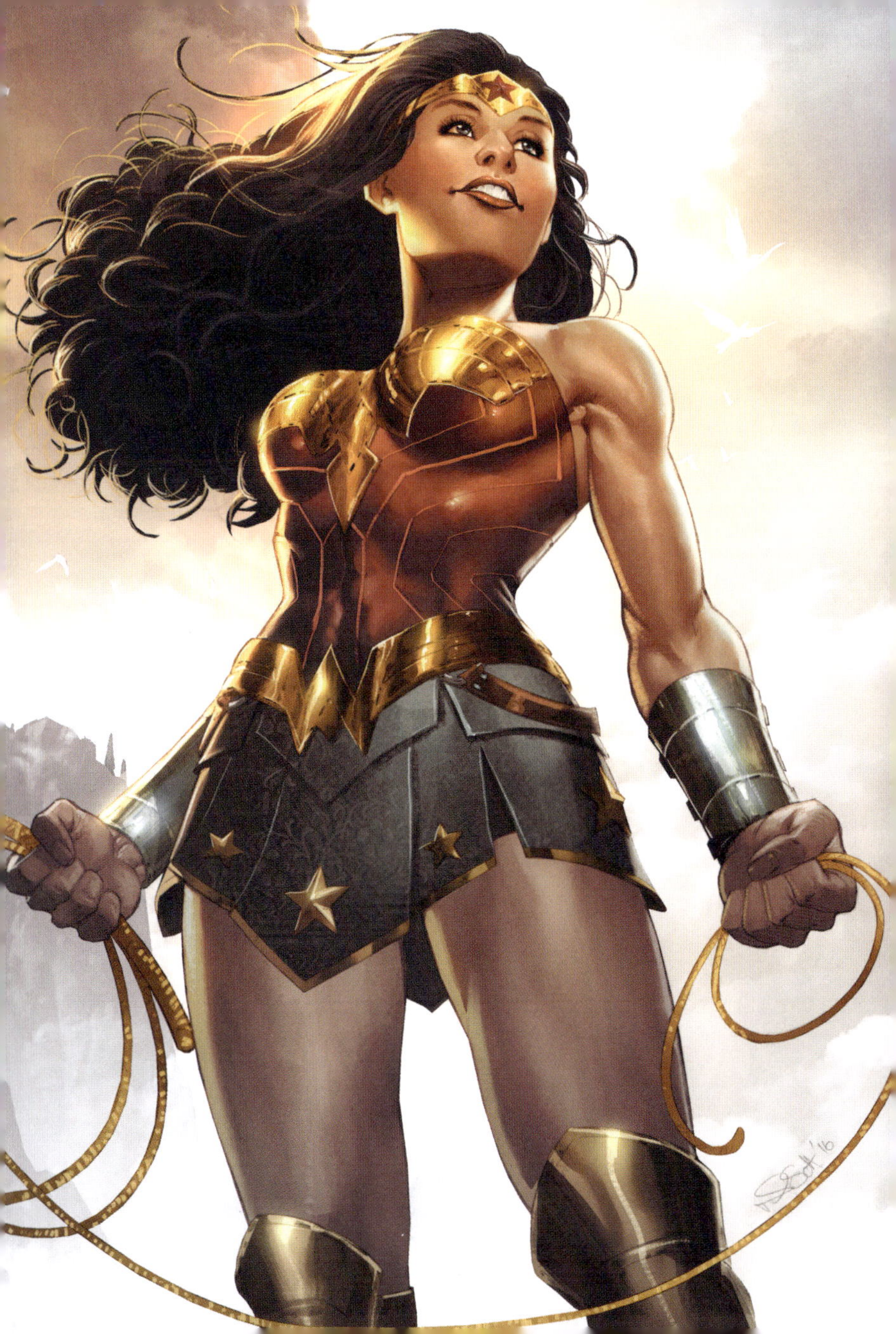